# DEBT

Poems / **MARK LEVINE**

# DEBT

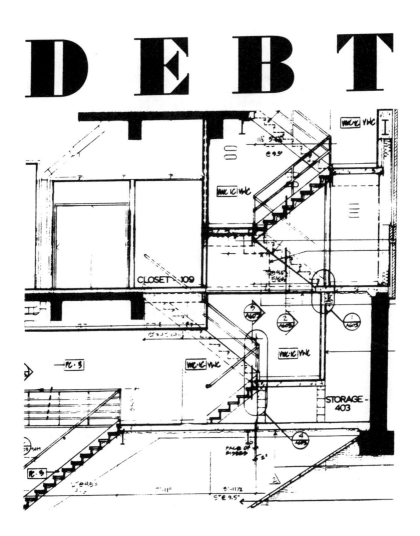

*William Morrow and Company, Inc. / New York*

It is the policy of William Morrow and Company, Inc., and its imprints
and affiliates, recognizing the importance of preserving what has been
written, to print the books we publish on acid-free paper, and we exert
our best efforts to that end.

Library of Congress Cataloging-in-Publication Data

Levine, Mark, 1965–
Debt : poems  / Mark Levine.
p.    cm.
ISBN 0-688-12397-X. — ISBN 0-688-12398-8 (pbk.)
I. Title.
PS3562.E8978D44    1993
811'.54—dc20
92-37862
CIP

Printed in the United States of America

First Edition

1   2   3   4   5   6   7   8   9   10

*For Evelyn Levine*

*1935–1985*

# *Acknowledgments*

Grateful acknowledgment is made to the editors of those publications in which the following poems appear: *The Antioch Review:* "Poem For the Left Hand"; *The Best American Poetry of 1991:* "Work Song"; *Black Warrior Review:* "The Polish Shoemaker," "Wild West"; *Boston Review:* "Debt," "Morning Song," "Battle Hymn," "The Polish Shoemaker," "Self-Portrait," "The Screen," "Disposal," "Currency Exchange"; *Colorado Review:* "Capitalism," "Notes on the Pyramids (I)," "Notes on the Pyramids (II)," "About Face (A Poem Called 'Dover Beach')"; *Cutbank:* "Seconds," "You"; *Denver Quarterly:* "Poem"; *The New Yorker:* "Work Song," "Sculpture Garden," "New Republics," "The Message," "Abstract Poem," "Statues"; *The Paris Review:* "At the Experimental Farm"; *Ploughshares:* "Mourning Song," "Debt," "Self-Portrait"; *The Threepenny Review:* "Occupied Territory."

Several poems in this collection have appeared in a limited edition, *Capital: Eight Poems,* from Windhover Press of Iowa City. My thanks to the publisher of Windhover Press, Kim Merker. And thanks to Ann Patchett for her help in preparing this manuscript for publication.

# Contents

### III

### *The Screen*

### IV

**DEBT**

# LANDSCAPE

I am caught at the end of a wooded cul-de-sac
in the glare of a light circling me.
I am holding a package tight to my damp body: the books
a friend has been asking for.
*Where does he live?*
Across the steel fence, across the canal that slices
the landscape in two?
—I haven't seen him in a long time.
He says he needs these books.
I ask a group of men who speak only in numbers.
It will be hard to stay long with my friend
in his harshly lit room. I am counting my steps aloud.
It is like speaking with him.

**1**

# AT THE

# EXPERIMENTAL

# FARM

My name is Henri. Listen. It's morning.
I pull my head from my scissors, I pull
the light bulb from my mouth—Boss comes at me
while I'm still blinking.
Pastes the pink slip on my collarbone.
It's OK, I say, I was a lazy worker, and I stole.
I wipe my feet on his skullcap on the way out.

I am Henri, mouth full of soda crackers.
I live in Toulouse, which is a piece of cardboard.
Summers the Mayor paints it blue, we fish in it.
Winters we skate on it. Children are always
drowning or falling through cracks. Parents are distraught
but get over it. It's easy to replace a child.
Like my parents' child, Henri.

I stuff my hands in my shoes
and crawl through the snow on all fours.
Animals fear me. I smell so good.
I have two sets of footprints, I confuse the police.
When I reach the highway I unzip my head.

I am a zipper. A paper cut.
I fed myself so many times
through the shredder I am confetti,
I am a ticker-tape parade, I am an astronaut
waving from my convertible at Henri.

Henri from Toulouse, is that you?
Why the unhappy face? I should shoot you
for spoiling my parade. Come on, man,
put yourself together! You want so much to die
that you don't want to die.

My name is Henri. I am Toulouse. I am scraps
of bleached parchment, I am the standing militia,
a quill, the Red Cross, I am the feather
in my cap, the Hebrew Testament, I am the World Court.
An electric fan blows
beneath my black robe. I am dignity itself.

I am an ice machine.
I am an alp.
I stuff myself in the refrigerator
wrapped in newsprint. With salt in my heart
I stay good for days.

# DEBT

That reminds me.
I read my name in the town ledger.
Workmen stare at me from their shovel blades.
It's out of the question, women won't touch me, they draw
    their nets
across their heads, they walk ahead of me a hundred yards.
Even now I am standing in paint.

I tried getting work. It's hard. They know me here.
They test my blood, they press my hands in ink,
they squint at my penis through smoked glass.
I swear oaths with a pencil in my mouth,
"I'm a company man!" I say.
They send a pound of butter to my doorstep.

It's you, they say. What is?
—I've been identified. It's him,
say the dentists, the children, the priests, say
an old Greek couple who claim I met them on a cruise.
I'm told my parents have identified me.
I have a familiar face.

I don't ask where I got these debts.
Some bad breaks here and there.
A glut in the pulp market. A poisoned horse.
Christmas, the recession, something or other

in the third world. I start taking
bets against myself.

The phone rings and they take it away.
They must put something in the water
to make it taste so good, like coconut.
Beneath my door they push their slips of paper
covered with Latin. They want to confuse me.
The sidewalks scrawled in Aramaic.

Reminds me. I go for walks at night.
The lit houses remind
me of a place I might have lived.
A man cracks walnuts under a yellow clock.
A woman, naked, counts her ribs.
I climb through bushes. Press my face to her window—
she looks at me like *maybe*, maybe
we did make love once but we can't be sure.

The Banker trails behind me with his abacus
and crowd of yes-men. I hear
the gold coins rub together in his vest.

The stoplights remind me. And the scars
on my ankles and the nails in my mouth.
Once my father pointed his finger at me.

Once my mother kissed me on the lips in winter.
I could have been a man like those men

on the roof, eyes narrowed at me
like diamond cutters. In surgical gowns
and crucifix tie clips, tight bands of wires
wound beneath their chests—
they remind me of me. All in sync
they cup their ears to the antenna.

Quiet. The Jew Levine is coming to collect
with his chisels and his sack of flesh.

## MORNING SONG

Hell's bells! Boss is at it again, splitting hairs with his
    penknife,
waxing his mustache. I read him the charts
while he shines his whistle, sneaking a look through the
    blinds—
the plague is right on schedule like a toy train.
His pals, and their wives, and the wives' lovers, and their
    lovers,
mill in the Green Room, having punched the clock.
They won't need their jewels any longer.

The moat is nearly done. That was one of my projects.
I can't complain. Boss has his moods,
but I know my value. He brought me home
from the Crusades. I'm a keepsake. He ripped the skin
off my family and kept that too. I remind him
of his mother, and his sister, and his son, and himself.
I bring tears to his eyes.
He's been to me like the father he killed.

Prussia is coughing. It's hard to sleep.
I give the musicians good reason to play on.

It's kind of nice to see everyone die
—but that's nothing new. Boss sits me on his shoulder.
The heaps of bodies grow like haystacks.
The haystacks burn. The horses run, forgetting their saddles.

*The riderless horses.*
Is it not the Christ is come?

Boss, how long did you think I'd wear the razor shirt
so you'd look at me and feel dangerous?
I've been watching you watching yourself on me.
I like what I see. I've learned some tricks.

Here I am ringing all the alarm bells!
Here I am lighting the ovens!
Here I am waking the guests, here passing out numbers!
Look, I've armed the corpses—they're angry, Boss,
they don't *feel* like talking.
What—am I your dream, that I can be
so many places at once? Am I your future?
Am I the teeth in your heart? Boss, wake up!

# BATTLE HYMN

I lie down in the hot sheep-pasture fog and wake up

chained to a dry-ice machine, dog tags chiming.
Down the street someone sorts pencils.
Someone is signing a contract for miles of sod.
Someone talks back to the camera. Someone

turns in his crib and is not someone.
I buy a face net from the man on the porch swing.
The killer bees are due by Memorial Day
which is no longer observed. The government spokesman

says *killer* is misleading.
He reads his statement from the rebels' compound,
the gun dangling just on-screen. He says his
tongue will be arriving in the mail.

Wait. Am I speaking or clearing my throat?
I get paid to stand with my mouth open.
The tape is rolling. I am *content neutral*.
Mine eyes have seen the glory. You—hands up!

Police with thick gloves point mirrors at me.
That's *me*? Just what do I think I am doing?
Answer: posing.
As what? A person? God? Something for sale?

The shoppers push by, stroking sheepskin and bird meat
and nerve gas and me. Prices rise and fall.
The Mayor's girl wipes fog from my Uzi.
My fatigues are half-full.

I am bought and divided and placed on the hearth.
Children clap their hands. I am a sing-along.
They unplug me and I keep running.
I change my morning teeth for my evening teeth.

# DOUBLE AGENTS

They knock on my door in whiteface speaking for God.

Go away, I say, I'm in bed
with my mother, I can't be disturbed. She denies it—
claims "bed" is a toddler's sand-pit; claims what we're doing
is molding a medieval fortress with plastic pails.
—She calls herself "Renée."
I touch her like The Flood, I touch her
like a vacuum cleaner. Fact is

I work both sides of the street.
Door-to-door I give my pitch, clutching my sample bag
like a fresh kill. Nine to five I bear witness

to Jehovah, he is the towel clerk at the Greyhound
men's room, stubbing
his cigarettes in the urinal. Sacred text confirms:
his private parts
are infinite. I make my route in a double

figure eight and return at night to the same
houses, concealed in glue and gabardine, selling my wares.
I speak so fast my teeth burn.
The housewives glisten.
I point the orange nozzle. I take away the stain
and its illusion.
Who among us does not crave the club

sandwich, salvation?
Late night I lay myself down.
I watch them come at me from all directions.
The traffic is not about to swerve around me tonight.
I twist myself into a double figure eight. I am very
calm.

Packed with tourists, the Greyhound speeds towards me.
Renée blows me a diesel kiss.
The TV cameras catch it all.

# SELF–PORTRAIT

Lying impatient for the burning copper thread

I wake next to me on the too narrow for two bedcage.

One of me his eyes squinched ankles crossed
I do not wake him he is scrawled with tubes.
One of me (me) a mess of broken glass circuitry sheet metal
   plastic
a fist-sized magnet. Hungry this morning and no mouth.

No one comes to change the scratched sheets.
They let the needles do the work the pumps.

I work quick not to get caught I steal glue and tools.
I take shape as I go along each step
unsure. It feels familiar suspenseful.
At last I see myself a box of sorts a picture window who am I
   kidding

—I am a TV. I buzz I receive everything.

Friends come to visit very somber wearing hats they stuff
towels in their mouths.
They seem bored one strums his fingernails on me.
They stand in a circle in my purple light I think they like
what I've become one even laughs eyeing the screen (me).

What do they see a woman eating coins they see
a dance contest sticks and flames
they see Europe carved up scraps tossed in the Volga
they agree it is good. They do not come too close
afraid of rays they do not recognize me.

The me on the bed they avoid
he makes a gurgling noise with each breath
he stinks very bad. I am not the man he used to be.

Late night I crawl back into bed very slow not to hurt
the one lying there hard flesh and cold.
I turn him I open his gown I am gentle God I do love him.
We make love the two of me like a beautiful machine
we are the finished product.

# MOURNING SONG

The proper word would be "ceded"—
I have gone completely over to the other side.
You wouldn't know me in my pressed brown
shirt and tie clip. You wouldn't know me with the white paste
swirled across my scalp.
Did you find me in the group picture I sent?
Row AA—a mile from the left?
I was the one with his thumbs crossed.

I was the one with his ribs labeled "Rio or Bust."
I'm glad to have joined the others.
Neapolitan song, pinochle, the barracks courtyard,
blood sausage, mice, fingers, tongue,
the ivory hair of the boy
who lies curled on his pallet: why?
Why can't the man-child return my love?

You were the life I had to leave.
It was too good.
How many people were taking their lives
because of us?
Now days are busywork—driving nails where they tell us,
sorting the bones into neat piles,
marking them in tiny calligraphic script. . . .
Do you have any idea how many bones in a single foot?
I try to learn such things, a bit each day.

Let me tell you what it's like to be nobody: it's good.
Last night I told my deepest secrets to a woman I hate.
A relief.
She laughed. Pounded her fists on the ground.
Today she'll tell everyone.
I've had enough of blame.
I took blame like a prisoner taking his rations,
sparingly with his tongue to the metal plate
for years. Until he gives in; until he speaks.

Oh love, it's love that's dead, not me.
Who thinks only the living speak? No, love, no,
it's only the dead.

Scratches on my stomach and no fingertips—
I come to in a calm
Jew terror, bandages strewn across the floor
in yellowed swirls. My eyelids
sticky. Bottles of sand lining the walls. Smell of fresh tar.

Who left these boots at the end of my bed?
Heels nailed with zinc. Laces winding
through thirty-six rivets. Whose uneven
footsteps above me? Is one of my legs shorter?
Is one of my legs hollow, like cork?
Who replaced my legs with these boots?
Oh what has become

of Grandfather, the Polish shoemaker?

I scrape my forearm with a plastic disk.
The blue numbers flake off
in wax shavings. I scrape down to the bone.
A small mound of shavings
softens under the light bulb.
I mold a figurine, etching the features with a pin
between my teeth. Bright green eyes, forehead thrust forward,
a sliver for a tongue, eight fingers—when it hardens
it looks like a Jew. A Jew
shoemaker Pole. It looks like me.

I scrape the soft part of my thigh and gather wax
for forty Jews—carpenters, tailors, craftsmen
all. They are wearing silk ties. Their capped teeth glitter.
From my foreskin I carve
twelve delicate, thin-lipped infant Jews.
Set them kneeling in the twelve corners of my room.
They face Jerusalem, they face God's black tongue. My

grandfather. My boots. My body. My scratches. My dozen
    Jews of piety.

The Jews multiply like Jews.
I separate the men from the women. Young from old.
I start piling them. They grow
anxious, they rub their padded shoes across the floor
streaking wax. Some men circle me:

sharp teeth, sharp fingernails. What of me
is left to attack?
To make more of them is to make less of me, Grandfather—

I am down to my boots.
I used up muscle long ago, and fat. Skin for the women.
What's left is bone, a bad texture.
It makes ugly Jews.

I resemble them more than they resemble me.

They are crawling in and out of boot-deep Poland.

Of my final scraps, my lips,
I shape a big, gleaming, broad-hipped man—
almost American. Wide hands, thick blond hair. To the Jews
I say he is sent from God. Your gift to me,
shoemaker—is it not God's body? You and me and God—
are we not the raw materials?

I clip your bootlaces into tiny wicks and feed them into
the cupped wax hands of the Jews.
My American holds a match on his tongue. Passes the flame
mouth to mouth with a long kiss.
The room smells smoky, like love.
Even the American smolders.

# SCULPTURE GARDEN

### 1

I won't speak for everyone. But my father, not
sleeping for six weeks, turns
into the crumbling Czar-on-horseback
statue in the central square of his birthplace.
He just stands there, life-like.
Didn't he listen? He wasn't supposed to look

back while escaping. Everyone died.
The bodies spread around the statue like linked cobblestones.
They died. He didn't. *It wasn't his fault.*
Why am I looking at him like this?


### 2

This is the house my father tried to build.
That patch of dirt raked
in geometric planes is a Japanese garden.
Those gaps the pigeons roost in are French windows.
The step-ladder, a spiral staircase, a helix. My father hasn't

slept in six weeks. There is a crack in the living-
room wall. There is an icy roof.
He is watching the plaster.
Certain the house will collapse.
Should I talk to him when he doesn't talk back?
His tongue coated white.
Should I touch him? He is dirty.

### 3

I can't help it.
When I think of that house I think of—.
The wreckers taking it down in ten minutes.
Neighbors carrying off faucets and two-by-fours.
My mother in drugged sleep with a ten-syllable disease.
A *galloping* disease.
My father next to her, his cracked lips the only moving thing
in sight.

### 4

What did they find with their shovels,
the Americans?
Was the thing stacked very high? Was the thing
visible from a single angle?
Did they have to walk around it,
the thing?

### 5

Hold still, my father says. The shutter clicks.
And again. My mother and I blink.
Pose after pose around the sickbed. White spots.

Once in a dream I made love to my mother.
It did no good.

**6**

I sit in my room hands blackened with newsprint.
Why not believe the papers.
Things turning wrong.
Gets in the dirt gets in the water.


**7**

Gets in the dirt gets in the water.

# POEM FOR THE LEFT HAND

Like Ravel's left-handed pianist, as long as there's a stage
I'll keep my back turned. Don't worry. I carved out a face
on the back of my head, filled with capped teeth, crooning
erotic secrets. My cup runneth over,
staining the keys. I can't find a sleeve

wide enough to hide what's missing, so I hire
an orchestra. This is my début.
I'm keeping my five fingers crossed.
Am I "less whole" than before? Yes,

not exactly. There's a family tradition of being
left-handed and bowing out early. Tonight I am
very early. The audience shifts in its seat,
staring at me through its rolled-up program, coughing
between movements. I try not to move. I try

not to. What little control I have
over my lost parts! I did not mean to, but
my dreams are taking a turn
for the real, like the rock thrown through my window
or the woman I saw burying herself.
Oh Lord, I runneth over and away

from myself, dragging a sack of piano scores
torn between the clefs. I have been whispering
in my ear, and I don't like the news. One hand

doesn't know what the other is doing.
I'm like the drowning man who lifts
his arm for the rope and goes straight under.
Down here, I can see myself talk—
the words floating to the surface
before I can grab them back. I'm all that's left
behind, half of me. I shall not want.

# AT THE EXPERIMENTAL FARM

### 1

They love me.
Each morning they fill the strongbox
in my chest with grass
and salt pellets—I have good hallucinations.
I think I am a caterpillar. I think I am
a wall. They spray me with anti-freeze, they turn me
each spring, I watch the buds spread open.

Up in the Big House they eat sugar all night making plans.
Their color pictures glow.
Their pointers glow.
Their crates of bones stamped with glowing rows of numbers
glow. What will their next move be?
What is the cause of this uncomfortable delay?

I hear them talk about me
night after night. I am the sum of what
they say about me.

### 2

The old dance begins again.
I think I am. I think I am.
I scrape myself free, the moon gleaming down
like a bottle cap. I brush cement from my hair.
When will this thirst go away, this powder on my tongue
like sand or garlic?

I make my way past the Big House, keeping low.
One last look at them—naked beneath white coats,
clumps of straw glued on their stethoscopes.
I bark at them with hate and desire.
One never forgets the first time.

One never forgets.
Oh peel off my electrodes—dig the wires
from the palms of my hands—what am I
when not monitored?

**II**

## ABOUT FACE
### (A POEM CALLED "DOVER BEACH")


It's dead out here. The sea is calm tonight.
Just me, the sand, the sand-like
things, wriggling like wet pockets.
I cover my eyes with some fingers; I have fingers
to spare. I open my mouth and hear the medicine
splashing on my tongue. The cliffs of England stand.

Behind enemy lines? Yes. Toujours. The Sea of Faith
was once, too, at the full. The barricades are stacked
like empty chairs after tonight's performance.
Is tonight's performance over?
I'm dragging bodies along as decoys, a dozen
well-dressed bodies, greasy, glazed with red sauce. Tonight's
   menu:
Peking duck. My stench is making me hungry.
Commander, may I have a body too?

Is someone quaking in my boots? To fear? Perchance, to flee.
Out here "advance" looks a lot like "retreat."
My wheels kick up sand as they spin.
Listen! you hear the grating.
My gears are caught. No use hurrying.
Time's nearly up. And I have
thoughts to collect, faces to grow.

My instructions read: "Come as you
were, leave as you are." Only, from the long
line of spray—

Commander, can you hear me?
I'm waiting for my answer.

Come to the window. Sweet is the night air.
My guests are here, clamoring to be let in.
I am here, clamoring to be let in.
*In*. Where is that? Come to the window.
Knocking twice, I greet myself at the door and am
surprised.

Oh naked shingles of the world. My enemy's skin is bad
from eating boiled soap and scrubbing with potatoes.
My enemy's parts are detachable.
He is having a reaction to his medicine:
pain-free, confused. Am I

my enemy's enemy? My enemy's keeper? My
enemy? Ah, love, let us be true.
We're all a bit tired
to be killing so much, but we continue.
The tickets were bought through the mail long ago so why
    not.
No time to save face.

Action. Action.
A cardboard bomber flies by with its flaming nets.

We are here as on a darkling plain.
Make me an offer. I'm going fast.
The theater is so crowded no one can be sure
if the fire is in their hair
or in their wigs.

# POEM

### 1

The soldiers torched the crops while retreating.
It only seemed fair.

### 2

Not much grows here anymore. Except bodies.
Everyone loves a parade.
*Look at the bodies*—wriggling in the field,
eating their way into the ground.
Their blisters make smacking noises.
It sounds like an aviary here.

### 3

They prop open my mouth with splinters.
They carve their initials on my thighs.
Their placard hangs from my cock.
Their time clock ticks at my feet.

### 4

I smell gas. Oh Jesus, tell me how you

### 5

do it, the wars fought on your charcoal skin,
the soggy heaps, burnt uniforms, drums, receipts,

megaphones.
You don't scare them away, do you? You attract them,

## 6

isn't that it? Honey, not ash? Even now?

## 7

Where is the spot on your body where I'm planted?
Which dead cell of you holds the silvery image
of this corpse field? A tender spot?
Your eyelid perhaps? May the pressure hurt.

## 8

"To save the village
I had to destroy it"—isn't that the right thing
to say? Those villagers dug my stake
straight through the belly of a woman
who—who knows—might have been my mother.
She screamed, Jesus, all of us scream
but you. I had to tear her apart to free her.

### 9

*Look at the ravens*—strutting, choosing
which of her or me to peck at first.

### 10

I drank my radium today. It's made me brave
as the lightning rod between my teeth.

All morning him circling in the steak-red limo, radio
squawking, crèche on the dashboard. With each pass
he shouts a lower price. I hold out for awhile.
I hold out for awhile.
When I nod he throws me a shovel and torch.

He opens the door. I see the rabbit
on his lap. His pink knuckles caught in the thing's ears.
A metal brace around his neck. A buzzing
sound from under his hat, like wet phone lines.
I sign the forms. I sign the forms.
He throws me some coins and steps on my fingers
with his meat-boots.

I wake next day on a red tiled floor.
The flames on my arm keeping the dogs back.
I watch the others winding past me to work,
toting chisels and wax-paper bundles.
Winding past my arm to the smokestack.

Loudspeakers everywhere: his voice pushing through the
    compound
like a wire, saying "God is great" and "Arbeit."
When I ask his name the violinists stop.
Women in peau de soie linger by his tent.

Roll call. He stands on the scaffolding with his printout
and aides. He laughs into the mike.

We laugh back. Chains rattle. We laugh back.
He dabs his fingers in sacred oils
and forces them into his mouth.
The sky is green with blackbirds.
He reads his list. "The world is made of sand and water."

# CAPITALISM

It's a kind of reflex, taking the fall.
If you listen closely you can hear me.
The flier says
*Put your ear to the page, get let in*
*on a secret.*

Giselle has wires looped round her ankles and wrists.
It's me who is her choreographer. It's me working
the cranks.
I learned from playing with wind-up toy soldiers
on the edge of the table.
*Rat-a-tat.*
I learned from the wind-up soldier.

I've sat in the kitchen
too long.
My eyes get hot and wet and I start
making up reasons—
"Indifferent Nature" or "Thirty
days hath September."

I'm not ready to go.
Time's up and I want
to stay.
I'm stamping my feet, pasting bread in my ears.
The buzzer continues.

Giselle has forgot what it's like
to move.

She just hangs there, getting fed, her joints swelling
some, but not bad.
"Giselle," I say—I am rubbing her with a butterfly net—
"The train needs its coal, and coal is a lot
like diamonds."

I am bending my knees when I speak. More a shovel
than a lover.

Giselle invokes the nineteenth century.
She thinks her wires are
invisible wires.
She thinks her wires are wings.
She will not be compared to a summer's day.

But Giselle—
Does the War Machine not love you?
Are you not crammed with things
that the War Machine needs? Are your people not
a hungry people?
Do officers not bang their heels on the dining-car table?
Is the name of this dance
not *Giselle*?

Stay as you are, Giselle,
thinking of Nature, thinking of
God.
Forget that it's me that winds you up.

The Industrial Revolution is dreaming, Giselle.
There are more of you where I come from.

# NEW REPUBLICS

### 1

It was the French Revolution all over again.
Wake before dawn—nab a good corner—Boss

troops by on stilts patrolling my cart:
tight stacks of walnuts, grapes pink side down.
Cut your hair, he says. I lop off his skull.

Look at me now, in my hero's robe,
whisked to exile in the back of an oxcart
spread with figs and bay leaves and—Mathilde,

her fingers wound in my hair. Versailles goes to hell.
Robespierre licks me. I can hardly keep up.

Maman, where is my costume?

### 2

My return: I am borne through the Arc
on tusks. I admire the handsome new scaffolding.

Heads line the streets. What is the sky doing
over there, behind the woodpile? It is year

Zero. The countdown begins.
The whistle vendor swallows.

### 3

*Nostalgia, you are an ancien régime—*

that's the song they play at my Gala.
They drink to my health. I sign contracts.

Is it time for me to see my thoughts?
Is it time for me to see my name in print?
The Censors kneel against the wall. The First Estate

trips on my hair; everyone laughs.
I think I'll laugh before I die.

I think I'll streak my hair with pomade.


### 4

Where are you, Mathilde? Those oaths I swore
your bastard father, do they count?
Do they count in the New Republic?

I don't like what this is
becoming. Speeches, speeches, strangers

grabbing each other in the street, taking pledges.
So I flee,

which is easiest.
Someday, on some calendar, this day will be

"The Past." Bygones. Sleeping dogs.
But not today. I feel it growing,
my hair, and I know not what that means.

And I like not that.


### 5

Not for nothing did Maman have me christened

*Etcetera.* Not for nothing does Don
Quixote pull up to my post, hands between legs

clutching his horse, crying for blades. I fear
I fear my head.

Yes,

he wears a windmill under his Spaniard's cap.
Yes, he makes a clucking sound; he told me so.

Oh Sun King! oh Mathilde! oh gentle Robespierre!—

I eat the Don's heart with a ballpoint pen.
The hair is hanging in my eyes real bad today.

# WILD WEST

*Loyalty?* Well . . . when the black and gold
rot kept creeping up Sancho's arms
like a wet sleeve, truth is I was afraid to kill him.
I let him ride the nag. Buzzards overhead.
The law on our ass. I bought him a mouth
organ to drown out his moans. I stole his hand
mirror and buried the pieces.
Late night I let him hug me—

He knew it had to be done. I poured booze all over him.
Pulled a money bag over his head, drawstring tangled.
Uncoiled the thick braided ropes.
This will sting, I said.
I pulled off his arms like fly's wings.

Now I ride the nag and he trails along
wearing my holsters. He nods when I've said nothing.
"Partner," I say. But I won't touch him.

He makes a good decoy. Trains stop for him.
Once he was trigger-happy; now, a conversation piece.
He hears me talking about him to myself
like an accountant. I sold his arms
to a traveling show. You need hands to count cash

so he and I don't talk business anymore.
He takes long walks in the cactus grove, muttering

"bountiful God." I've seen him eyeing my guns.
How did he stuff those spent shells in his pants?

He always thought it was in my mind
when we shot up a town, dumped lime in the wells,
drove the livestock from one fire to another.
Now he knows. Now he
knows. I was playing along with his playing along.
The enemy's real,

partner. I think it's me. I blindfold him
and spin.
I put a poker to his ankle.
I make him write the word *gunpowder*
in the dirt with his jaw.
I hug my saddle when he explodes.

## CURRENCY EXCHANGE

"Do not cry, little tart" is the song I wake singing.
Shall I tell you my dream of the blue elevator?
Shall I lather my babies? Shall I make love?
Shall I open a store with shelves and clerks?
Shall I scrub myself with a gum eraser?

So Claude holds my place on the bank line
in his holy-day suspenders.
I give him a slice of smokestack and jam.
Claude, I say, do not blame the railroad. He repeats:
"Klaus in the onion patch, spade in hand.
Mama in her apron, filled with wax and sand."

Who's afraid of doors and walls?
I fall to my prayer mat in the marketplace.
Children splash in a sheet-metal basin.
Somersaults, backflips, gas chambers, cartwheels.
I buy a turnstile and a bell-shaped hat.
I rinse my teeth.

The Chancellor in his radio talk talks of soccer camps.
I kiss his needle-nosed eyes.
How long will he sleep in his wooden cart?
Is this a matter for family to decide?

So I bring my daughters plaster-cast horses
with bright red wheels. I bring them hormone shots.

Because we walk in the forest with water jugs.
Because my daughters grow pregnant like envelopes.
Do we take the day off? Do we?

Claude and I dance with the line of Brink's trucks,
Claude with his needle in his pocket.
Claude goes too far.
The crowd stamps its feet in the Stadium, and yes:
I lift my hat. I point my dogs.
Claude's mouth fills with traffic and armbands.

We dip him in Jew-tar. We roll him in Eastmarks.
We hammer our clogs on the bell-shaped pavement.
Klaus twirls and swings Mama's oxygen tank.
A kiss is still a kiss.

# OCCUPIED TERRITORY

## 1

It seems it happens over
night, like "The End of the Stone Age" or the three
wooden shoes I find in the alley, one painted with a green
   bird.
The others left this morning when I was asleep.
They left in a wooden cart.

Because of my bad foot I've been excused from duty.
It's just me here now. Me and my radio.
In other news: the cotton gin.
I drink ice water from a tube and stay in bed late,
waiting for curfew. Today the pilgrims

parade through town in their steel-blue suits.
Jeeps trail alongside, trailed by dogs and cargo
trucks piled with baggage. The marchers walk barefoot.
I hear them swallowing. Not far now
to the cave with the shallow red stream.

This sketch—a bull raised on its hind legs, a blackbird
with open black wings—has been translated as
"The Hittites came and burned the fields."
Out back: women with sheets and rocks.
When I hurry through the gravel streets on market day

my hurrying sounds like a jackhammer.
In other news: the Army barber found

in an alley, his mouth stuffed with batteries.
All night the trains pass on the newly laid tracks.
Who has seen the orange flashes in the desert?

I get headaches. Overnight three more

## 2

houses have disappeared, one painted with a green bird.
Who has seen? The Army displays a cache of spears with tribal
    markings.
I dream of sheets nailed to the window, I wake coughing
but I don't get up. I dream of elevators.
How shall I put it? My clubfoot:

like dragging a sandbag up a metal stepladder.
Everyone hears me coming.
My foot has been sending me messages, like *swallow the
    mouthpiece.*
Bulldozers pass on the freeway, headlights blinking.
Another tomb unearthed, this time Third Dynasty.

I'm looking for remains. A body. I'm looking for bodies.

Once the Army lived across the street, playing
as schoolchildren, playing in the gravel and wood chips.
The teachers posed as teachers. I got used to it.

The Army came by my window at night, picking through trash
for empties. Targets. Each target assigned

a code name, like "Elijah." I swept up the glass the next day.
The Army moved in upstairs. The Army moved closer.
Closer and closer. The Army moved into my radio
and moved on. The Army moved into my head, my mouth,
and I tasted the Army and I swallowed the Army.


### 3

I've lost my inhaler. Look: men with shovels.
For six days digging in the shadow of the oil wells.
On Monday our ballots are collected and counted.
The pit filled in and covered with tar.
Private planes land there, marked with tribal markings. In

other news: the satellite dish. The microwave oven.

Once I was white and then I was black.
It happened overnight. The Army is advancing inside me,
sprinkling lime on the thing in the street, the thing
inside the burning tire. In other news:
the Berlin Olympics. The Doctor

injects dye in my foot and watches his screen.
I dream of aerosol. It's raining.

"My people"—what a thing to say! "My people live
by the transmitters and have started beaming messages to
   space."
You don't believe? In what? I'll tell you

what happens overnight: the pyramids.

## NOTES ON THE PYRAMIDS (II)

Want. Want. Want. Want. Want. He sends
gloved messengers with gifts for me,
green and blue birds, glass tubes. All night
him pacing in the bell tower, binoculars raised, looking
at me. He takes me to the pyramid.

All the signs agree: "It's nearly done."
His mouth is dry. His mouth is wet.
He names a day for me. He cuts his chest with stones
for me.
I wear his stained shirt.

Nearly done. We run out of sand for mortar.
The cement trucks stand in the lot like
monuments, weeds growing under the wheels.
The smokestack is quiet. The digging stops.
He doesn't know what to do. He's looking at me.

I tell him to give it just one more day.
I tell him not to make the firstborn decree.
I try.

I try.
A few more stones left to raise.
We stand at the base of it, him with his rabbit.
We stare at each other pink-eyed, my arm
around his hot neck. I say his name.

I say his name.

The pulleys pull between us, setting in place
the last flesh stones. Each of us holds
the other's starred birth papers.
My God, what we've got on each other.

# ABSTRACT POEM

On one side of the plaza we build a replica
of the Holy Ruins, spraying the sand
with white paint. Across the way
some younger men trace a ring of orange ditches
by lamplight. Twice daily at the edge of the woods
the spokesman issues denials, clarifications,
detailed booklets printed on textured paper.
The radio plays chamber music and dance-hall songs.
Breakfast is biscuits and coffee.

There are times when it seems best to stay
outside the plan. I'd rather not know
what it is I'm doing. It's very quiet here now
that the road is paved and the road crew taken
off the job. Even the sky is quiet.
Trucks coming through at night don't stop.
The air from the west smells like vinegar.
Powdery white spots have begun to appear on us.

We don't care.
We go to our tents, we smoke, we wash our shirts, we
chase rabbits through the snow, we get tired.

I'm tired of counting. How many is enough?
How many fingers drumming on metal plates?

I can't shut the timer off.
They'll wait—won't they? I'll never finish counting.
How many chalk marks on the blue slate now?
The field where we cut down the trees
is filling with snow.

# WARRANT

By midnight I get over it. I start hammering again.
The guards stand by the fire pit, burning papers.
So many numbers, so many names.
Hammer gently, they say: we're trying to think.

The guy next to me can't stop coughing.
The guy next to him can't stop singing "Glory to God
in His sacred groves."
When is this going to stop?
The ovens stay lit all night. Everything sounds the same
when it burns, like newsprint, like the telephone book,
like name, rank, number, date of birth.
Once I start talking, what's there to stop me?

When I run out of nails I hammer pens.
Ink stains the wood the color of my tongue.
I don't need my pens anymore. They know it was me.
They can sign my name to anything
and they won't be wrong.

# STATUES

We cannot say anything we want to say
until we are fed the white paste
and the planks have been carefully laid,
giant cranes gliding behind us.
The flow from the gray pump continues.
We slip in the wet grass.

After a five-minute break we return, now
with chrome tags nailed to our belts.
We have removed the statues and divided them.
We have not yet found the list.

The list, when found, will be folded in sections
of uneven length, called "stripped shelves"
or "rooms beneath the childhood home."
I am still waiting for the white horse

to return, which I lost
while holding a yellow bird to my chest.

We sit as still as our reflections
like people gripping the wing of an airplane
waiting for the airplane to stop.
How the landscape changes from hour to hour.
Black hills, gravel pits, train tracks, fields
surrounded by rotting fences.
There are no reasons. Here we are.
We would like to start moving the statues.

**III**

# THE SCREEN

# INTERVENTION

## 1

So saith the Speaker, to open this performance:

"Our guiding assumption had been that The Line in the Sand
was fortified by God with steel jaws
and poison pellets, lilac bushes disguising
the Arabian palsy. Who would we choose to get close enough

to look? Each time we neared, the sirens rang,
calling us to prayer. By now it's clear. The Bosses
were in on it too, in the name of 'Common Good.'
Only an accident revealed that The Line

had been engraved by our own repetitive
actions, including: 'The Long March'
in which the Leaders took such pride; the continuous
punching of time cards; the movement of pens scratching our
    names

onto this contract and that form; the ridges we made
inserting coins into narrow slots, waiting endlessly
for our call to go through. *We made The Line.*
Say it: *It is our Line.* What do we do now?"

Reader, Customer: join me.

I just got my handout. I think I lied on the form.
Across the street, a line stretches past the corner,

sleeves rolled up for the vaccine.
I don't want to catch what they've got, or will get.

Isn't it too late for that? For "Best Wishes" or "Yours,
Sincerely"? Isn't it too late for "Sincerely"?

A man with leaflets starts working the line,
saying, "In these times, our country needs us to stand up

and be counted." What are "these times," and why aren't they
over yet? My legs, my names, my souls are tired

of being counted. I take enough pills of different sizes
to pluck my head far from my body's reach. My reply:

"The head, properly speaking, is an ornament, the icing
on God's rotting biscuit." Don't look now, Partners

in this Poem, but I think we have said the wrong thing.
The Government has stolen my mask, and my skin

is a fiercely decorated, flaming banner.
You would not know it by looking at me, but

I am naked. You would not know it by touching me.
Today's entrée at the Embassy Canteen

is frosted Double Bind, served with lettuce and soup du jour
on a starving platter.


### 3

It's sexy the way we all talk at the same time

About so many different things, like snakebites

And thunderstorms, like Persian rugs. I could go on. It's
    Democracy.

It's sex. We agree on nothing but the eighty-eight keys

Of Glenn Gould's grand piano. By sheer

Coincidence, eighty-eight parties are vying for a single decisive
    vote

In next week's election.

Do we dare vote for ourselves? Against ourselves?

Why can we not do both? You will know me when you see me.

I am, at bare minimum, a two-headed monster.

Intent on reproducing by artificial means.

# THE ELECTION

Those of us with resources don't need hints.
We gather at Jack and Trudy's to watch the returns.
Jack's put his chips on the dark horse at 8 to 1.
I can barely see his scars beneath his name bracelet.

Each of us holds in the hand not on our laps
a pearl-handled knife to slice fruit, and a brass
spit for dipping. My fruit: seedless tomatoes,

which toast well over spruce chips. "Pine nuts,"
says Trudy, "are a figure of speech."
I can't nod since my accident.

What was it we voted for today, in our long black robes?
Jack used a blunt pencil, and I went downtown by electric bus
to pull the levers in a booth smelling of dog hair.

Autumn. Jack wanders room to room, changing light bulbs,
nailing cardboard over the safety plugs.
His robe hangs slightly open.
He says, "Someone, not God,

is sitting in the parlor with an electric board game on his lap."
Jack has had a series of dreams about Man Ray

that he suggests would make a lively poem. Jack's fruit
is moonberries, washed down with herb butter bathed in light.

Should you be relieved? No: this isn't made up.
Jack is an "Idea Man" at a large firm.
Trudy runs a bookshop and wants to edit children's books
on the side. Convinced? Fact is
I fucked them both, years ago, and I am trying
to write a shorter, more realistic poem. Fact is

Jack and Trudy are my parents. We live in a house
built on the model of an acoustic guitar
once owned by Andrés Segovia.
The blue pool hasn't been skimmed in ages.
Trudy's fruit

is cocktail shrimp flambé, a pun
on "fruits de mer." Often, late at night, we play a word
game called *Ritual*, Jack holding a steel basin
to catch whatever may.

At this point, somebody ought to die, but doesn't.

"When the election ends," says Trudy,
"it'll all be clear,
like a lake without any water."
I want to nod. I've had an accident.

Outside the glazed window, a boy with a wrinkled head
or hat shouts "Give it back!"

When was the last time I felt like that?
An hour ago, when I started this poem? Now? Next week?
The blood drive is over, leaving empty parking spots.

Tonight I shave in public for the first time.
Ladies and Gentlemen, do I have your attention?

It's tiring, all this wondering what to do or think.
Jack says "This is getting too big for us."
His operation was a publicized success,
the radio says he will live
for thousands of years.

The holding room where we've come to be processed
reminds our host of the temporary chapel at an airport,
except for the small fires down the hall
where the crew burns its uniforms after the last bell.

So quiet. *Have* all the planes dropped from the sky?
"Acts of God" are in progress. That much we know.
Patiently we file our claims, join the paid staff
in waiting for the blue smoke. I feel "virtuous,"

and I don't mind saying so. My chair, bolted to the floor,
reminds me of (a) gravity and (b) childhood.
One row over, the old man stops tapping his foot.
When will *my* number come up?

We would all lodge complaints, but we haven't any.
In this way our host is right: we *are* family.
The Pope's removal adds suspense to the chain of events.
Will I go to bed with anybody tomorrow? Is the drawing

taking place at this moment beneath a decorated khaki tent?
What will his or her name be?
Or is it me?
Look at the line I just wrote: "Neither a borrower

nor a borrower be." The consensus is we're all prone
to lose our hands in our back pockets

moments before the double doors fly open for the last time.
Day by day the receptionist here changes place

with her telephone bank, all the buttons brightly lit.
She has stopped taking reservations. When will she tell us
what we owe her? I've seen the way she hides
the receipts beneath her skirt. I've heard the pages

being turned, and turned, and turned.
Tonight's dinner joke is the Pope's head on a platter.
We watch the screen while we eat, taking turns with the
    antenna.
The show is called *Could I Be Anybody*

and can't be turned off by remote.
*Liar, liar.* There's no need to turn it off.
There's no remote.
The Master of Ceremonies calls the number of the player to
    my right

and they come for him across the magnetic field
with their pincers and oils and red robes.
I step in front of him to block their way.
They pull him right through me.

# AIR·TRAFFIC CONTROL

While I unpack my suitcase they arrive in one-piece
uniforms, clear plastic gloves. One unscrews the doorknob.
One steps up and counts my money and nods
and nods until they are all nodding.

Were they bored in the sand, I ask.
Are their mouths sticky?
I offer a lemon finger bath, or dried fruit
in the bowl by the pillow. One counts my cash.
They watch me undress on the hot strip of rug.
My clothes don't come off in one piece.

Outside: the barking, the shadows of airplanes.
I read from my list.

My list says: "Coughing, the body evacuates itself."
They tape orange tape on the rug and I stand there.
I hear my name called. I know that trick.
My list says: "Bring the boys

home. Spare no expense. The pellets are drying in the cellar
on the top plank. Bring the boys home. But only when
the time is ripe."

None of them wears a watch.
One of them unties a flour sack filled with crickets.

One of them says "The Lord is my Shepherd."
Two of them dog-whistle through their fingers. Two others
wrap a hot shirt around my eyes.

I am the client. I can pay my own way.
How do airplanes work? I have landed the craft
on water, on ice floes, I have stopped short of the glass
tower, breaking nothing. I get places. Yes. I'm in one

place, I'm in another place, in-between is a white streak.
Numbers. Headphones.
When it works, I'm not supposed to hear the motor.
Alpha, I've been hearing the motor.

So they arrive, stacking the canisters at my feet.
They paste their blue-green thread to my chest.
Am I holding out on them? From behind me
one pushes three glove-plastic fingers inside me,
pinches, finds nothing.

Who are they? Who are they? Air-traffic control
wants to know. Air-traffic control has been *thinking*
of me, and *wants to know* my position. Who are *they*?

I hear water boiling. I hear a slap.
Someone cries "Read it!" My head is sticky.

My list reads itself on TV: "The Sandman
is angry, he wants a refund. The troops are stacked
in pyramids." From this distance

the world looks like the carved bottom of a question mark.
I have seen the Sphinx and we have spoken of
"the future."
Adjust your antenna. That is me in your picture.
Carrying two trophies. For the two heroes I am.

# REQUIEM

Friday night. Dad's in for his valves.
Advance notice reveals that
"Isadora Duncan Is Among Us"

is the name of tomorrow's poem. Today's name is "Bev."
Dad's staff comes by
with handprints on their smocks, tamping their pipes
in Dad's bowl. "Borkum Riff," says Dad, "is creamy, mellow,
and tastes of the open sea." He speaks through the tube

in his trachea, and the staff, leaning forward,
hears only *Glug glug.* One of them unwraps
a crusted scalpel. The head man, I'm told,
is the one with his wrist dangling to his knee,
a pocket Bible in his pocket. I've found a new

elixir to keep me up at night: ground beans
from Sumatra, apple skins, forkful of gelatin.
Lately it's just me and the rattling windows.
Traffic stops and goes.
Traffic does *not* bleed. On Friday,

today, the Jewish kids scream from school, hours before dusk,
in their wine-black caftans. I set down my clarinet,
watch them stamp single file through the gutters,
clutching the lemon and the hollow stalk. I name them
"Robin" and "Leslie" and "Pat" and "Kim" and—

*Bev.* Bev, I've lost the "reverent posture."
This year's masquerade began at midnight.
My Latin Mass for boys and girls lies folded on the music
     stand,
black and red notes barely filled in.
Will Dad never dress up and scare us at night?

When I go to the Market the Holy Ghost trails me
with his orange extension cord, padded earphones.
I wake at dawn without the alarm
to see them brush the glaze on Dad's chest.
We all sign his paper gown with a wet black marker.
The Holy Ghost lunges at my ankles.

Now the vegetable stall's selling white buckets,
two for one.
Batteries are on special in the basement.
The grocer is no more a grocer

than me, the Princess of Avalon, testing this year's sweetmeats
before the labeling and packing of cans.
This movement
of the piece is scored for calliope and radio.
The Holy Ghost hits high C.

"Currency," says the notice, "must be exchanged at the
     border

for rubber bullets."
The Bureau tells me I've been detected.
I'm making that old-time noise again.
I confess. I confess

to wishing "everything" were not possible.
Roll 'em, says the cameraman. Cut, says Bev.
Action, says the Holy Ghost.

# SECONDS

The caption of this photograph is "Man hit by falling ice."
In the chapters that follow, the theory of the cosmic
second hand unfolds in layman's terms, with reference
to the sand dollar and DNA.
Is dinner ready yet? How long has dinner been ready?
Despite the sun, it grows warmer here each day.

The question remains: What *hasn't* been lost? Who made off
with the last poem—the one I was saving my all for?
I gave my itemized collection of used things
to the government, on the condition it be returned
with interest when "the need arises." I can't be sure
but I think the need is arising. Signs include: increased

appetite, bus trips to abandoned villages, prophetic
dreams in the third person, the composition of unresolvable
    fugues
for cembalo and God.
When will the mail truck arrive?
I belong to a club that each month gets sent splinters of the
    Sphinx
concealed in boxes of Syrian apples. The *real* Sphinx:

a shape with lion body and the head of a man.
Chapter 20 concludes: "In the future
it is theoretically possible that the head will be considered
a body part." Oh prophets of Babylon and Islam and Judea

in your studded necklaces of glass and bone,
hear me: I cannot see a "future"

for myself, or my double, or his double.
Where are you taking us with our written consent?
Will there be painted bars across the windows?
Will there be elections each Tuesday, and time clocks
surgically implanted in our glands?
I am here at your disposal to second the motion.


Surely this moment has been written by professionals with
    much to lose.
Surely it cannot go on much longer, the desert carnival.
"Surely"—did I say that? I can't remember what I said,
whether I said it, whether all along without my knowing
I have been speaking someone else's lines.
Someone small. Someone perfectly dangerous.

**IV**

# YOU

The screen goes blank. The thornbush on the blue
screen goes blank. A burning log drops
into the soggy peat. You: you can stop talking.

This whole production—costumes with silver stripes,
feathers, glue, wet tongues, skin
that looks like skin—you can stop it now.
The sawdust stage, the crooked red scaffolding.
You can practice stopping it.

Is anything moving in the dark? We close our eyes,
we listen to the fluttering sheets, the blue smoke—
Are we moving? With the darkness taken away,
can you move your legs? I can.
I would like to say something. The blue

thornbush has stopped speaking and burning.
The sun will not pass through the wet berries.
Men have set down their shovels
in flat lanes of cleared peat. The last
plane flies into the screen silently.

I would like to say the film was not allowed to end.
I throw up my hands: no scars.
No pictures fading across the flat lines
of my body, not even when we add
singed hair, a painted shirt.

On the white table I read the numbers printed on my pill.
On the white table I lie with my pill
beneath the light and the last remaining figures
in their white shoes. I listened

to your tape but could make out nothing
with the birds squawking in the background like
burning leaves. To see the drifting sheet—
coming down on the body
like a silent white bird with yellow eyes.
Coming down on the body like a body.

# INSIDE

You think that since the light goes on and off
behind the third-floor drapes, that since the phone
on the narrow sill rings twice then stops—
you think he is there? We think many things

about him. We sit as if on tiled rooftops
staring across the clothesline toward him.
His red sheets were dry until the rain made them white.
Each day the folded paper drops to the yard

and disappears at night. "He is of this world"
is a comforting idea. We think we see him
unpacking his briefcase, washing with soap.
The stacks of wood out back may be used to build

a fire; a ship; a sculpture; the lid of a box.
We think we have narrowed it down: the steel pail
with the scraps of blue paper where he scrawls
his messages is in the linen closet or behind

a wall panel he removes. Or he stuffs his mattress
with these jottings. Or his pillow. We can't sleep.
Whatever he does, we want him to stop.
The bruise on his thigh doesn't get smaller.

His yard is strewn with plums. We think of wine.
An old woman comes for him and they step

through a break in the fence.
They do not get cut on the rusted wires.

The noises coming from his room like wounded birds
turn out to be wounded birds.

# HERE

How cold it is inside. And yellow.
How I would like to light myself one more.
To taste it, hot, starting from the spiny bottom.
To rub my hands in it.

Here, the dirt grows wet beneath the plastic sheet.
A voice runs down my leg like a tongue.
The pictures have stopped changing, except
the picture of the burning house. Time "passes."
And every name here is a name for a thing,
like "pipe"—

You asked me where the cop came from. I said the poem
hailed him. The poem needed him, his glove,
his stick which could be used to prop the table.
He's gone now. And the empty road seems
to mean the traffic went too fast
into the field with the white trees.

Do you hear the wind? It has nowhere to go.
A poem that says otherwise is a lie.
What does it sound like inside of you,
beneath the blue flaps of skin where the air escapes
while your back is turned to the man with the drum?
We looked everywhere for the noise
and found nothing, just broken shells,
flakes of tar—

The cop left his hat behind when he left.
We took it as a sign. It kept us here.
We make our own clothes with what we find.
We have stopped keeping count. We have learned
to sleep with the grinding noise, the smell.

There are no such things as noises and smells.

# SONG

Would it be wrong to say the song the boy
is playing in his room across the street
is a "sad song"? He plays it over and over.
His shades are drawn. I've thought of several
sets of words to go to the song. Would it be
wrong to say it is a "child's song"?

Last night his father stood barefoot on my lawn
threatening me. All night I heard the apples
dropping to the sidewalk. The trucks came through
at dawn, then the paper boy with the paper
I didn't order. I read it. I counted to forty
holding my breath. I counted to forty again.

Today's chores: painting the roof red, watering the drive.
I read the twelve rules on the side of the can.
Last night I swallowed something I shouldn't have.
A piece of shell. Maybe a seed. It went down sharp.
This morning was "partly sunny." Now it's raining.
The red paint runs down the walls and windows.

So long as I stay put, the person at the door
can't see me and I can't see them. On TV
today I see a girl I knew a long time ago
in the crowd at a baseball game. It reminds me
of a phonograph I bought the year I knew her.
I couldn't say where the music is coming from.

Why can the weatherman not predict today's weather?
Why can the camera not predict today's news?
Is it wrong to call the boy's song "Mystery
for Mystery's Sake"? To watch the ballerina
dance her solo in her skin-colored body suit? To say
"She is an Argentine native living in Germany"?

# DISPOSAL

### 1

I have three minutes to get it done.
To get rid of it.
I need the proper tags, the glossy ones
sticky on both sides. The man out back

kneels in the cut grass, teeth chattering.
I cover him with a faded serape.
I wipe his mouth. He smells of cake.
Now I see him now I don't.

### 2

They have arrived to paint the floor
with yellow paint, and later to spray the grass.
I initial the pink pad on both sides.
Where does the smoke come from?

When the phone rings I talk.
It's always either my sister
or her sister or my lover or him again.
I don't care which. My mother

### 3

turned six yesterday.
She wasn't around to give gifts to.

Shall I make of myself un grand cadeau?
Sprinkled with rose water, dusted with sawdust?

I dropped something in the giant yellow leaves.
Are mine the only fingers moving in the dark?
It's not that I'm a "good" person or "bad" person.
My mother is too young to say "person."

# THE NAME

Taking measurements with red string. Pacing the wet
dirt littered with bottle caps, glass.
Filling a pail with dirt. Packing it.

Hearing the name called out at night.
Writing it down. Hearing it. Hearing spoons
struck across the wet doorknob.

We shoot the scene again and again.
Yellow light. Blue light.
This time I try without talking.

Lying in bed. Watching the door.
God? A rag doll floats above me, stuffed
with shredded paper beneath its dirty skirt.

"God?" I cannot write it down. Who is it
at night, whispering the name of the one
that lit the fire? I pour dirt on the ashes,

hot dirt. Who is it pulling at my blanket?
The rag doll floats above me with its dangling
red string, painted mouth painted open.

## ICE

The clock in the wall says one oh one three.
Wall slipping away, like a green car gone backward
down a long path lined with white stones.
The car sinks in the lake. We had thought the ice strong.
We had thought and the thought grew warm and soft.
We unbuttoned our coats. Our gloves were wet.
We unbuttoned our pants. A door was slammed.
The windows we tried to unlock were taken from us.
Our buttons dropped like bells to the tiled floor.

It is one oh one four. Let us not speak of walls.
There is a lack of weather here.
I wake in the middle of a stone-covered box
covered with the words
"Let us not ask *How many* but *How often*"
printed on its back.

I am looking for the bridge I took yesterday.
The elevator? The shovel? The woman?
A woman with a body beneath her coat?
When I touch her she moves away.
When I touch myself I move away.
The picture of today is the size of a postage stamp.
When you look closely does the locked door reappear?

# BOTH "A" AND "NOT-A"


The corpse revives. Let me tell you a story.
Chips of white stone are scattered in the courtyard.
Four long lines, each three deep.
Some in jackets, some in robes, some wearing bracelets,
some splashed with perfume, some smoking.
It is hard to speak above the footsteps

above the opening and closing of doors
above the broken glass being swept into bins.

Balloons are released in the distance.
A cloud of blackbirds drifts like a banner
and falls down. A child dances then stops.
There are four different levels of flame.
Hard to eat with the smell of burnt sugar
in the air, sticky patches of burnt sugar on the fence.

On the other side of the fence a story is moving.
There once was, et cetera.

# THE MESSAGE

Alone at last. With him.
Both of us bare-chested. His legs parted. Mine crossed.
Him wearing the hat I stole for him.
I've got the message he's been waiting for,
I tell him. Folded in a green book
in a stapled box in the green car.
I think he nods. I think

in the time it took to get here he changed.
He stares at me, the blue chalk in his fist.
He crumples something in his pocket.
I can't make him speak. I can't make him spin
by clapping my hands behind his head.
Night: the walls collapsing around us.

It takes a day to get here by car.
A day divided into many days
like an animal with dozens of drifting legs.

How did we get here? We played the radio.
We sat by a pit filled with rain.
A blue horse jumped in the tall grass.
We passed through a mile of yellow trees.
A man in the road wore one glove,
waving a flare. At the bottom of the hill
a car burned. Windows blackened and whitened.

The radio tells nothing of any of it.
Alone with him. His finger bleeding.
I could tell him the story of the day of
the storm, the wedding, the ripped shirt and
the broken window. All one long day
like a long high fence.

I'm not afraid of repeating myself.
He found me.
It's so dark I can hear his finger
pointing at me. Which is my cue.

## ABOUT THE AUTHOR

Born in 1965, Mark Levine grew up in Toronto and was educated at Brown University and the University of Iowa. His work has appeared in many publications, including *The New Yorker*, *The Paris Review*, *Ploughshares*, *The Best American Poetry*, and in a limited edition collection, *Capital*. He currently teaches at the University of Montana and lives in Missoula, Montana.